BABY HORSES

Baby Horses

Photographs by William Muñoz
Text by Dorothy Hinshaw Patent

Dodd, Mead & Company • New York

Lovingly dedicated to Sandy
and all her babies that
give her so much joy.

Acknowledgments

The photographer and author wish to thank the many
people who generously allowed their horses to be photo-
graphed for this book.

Text copyright © 1985 by Dorothy Hinshaw Patent
Photographs copyright © 1985 by William Muñoz
Distributed in Canada by
McClelland and Stewart Limited, Toronto
Printed in Hong Kong by South China Printing Company

1 2 3 4 5 6 7 8 9 10

Library of Congress Cataloging in Publication Data

Patent, Dorothy Hinshaw.
  Baby horses.
  Summary: Describes the activities of foals in their
first months of life.
  1. Foals — Juvenile literature.   2. Horses — Parturition
— Juvenile literature.   [1. Horses.   2. Animals —
Infancy]   I. Muñoz, William, ill.   II. Title.
SF302.P37   1985   636.1′07   85-1573
ISBN 0-396-08629-2

Contents

Beginnings

Most horses are born in the
springtime. The baby, called
a foal, is wet.

The foal's mother licks it. This helps fluff up its hair and dry it.

The foal tries to stand up a few minutes after it is born.

Standing isn't as easy as it looks.

The mother checks on her baby
to make sure it is all right.

The foal tries again to stand.

This time, it succeeds.

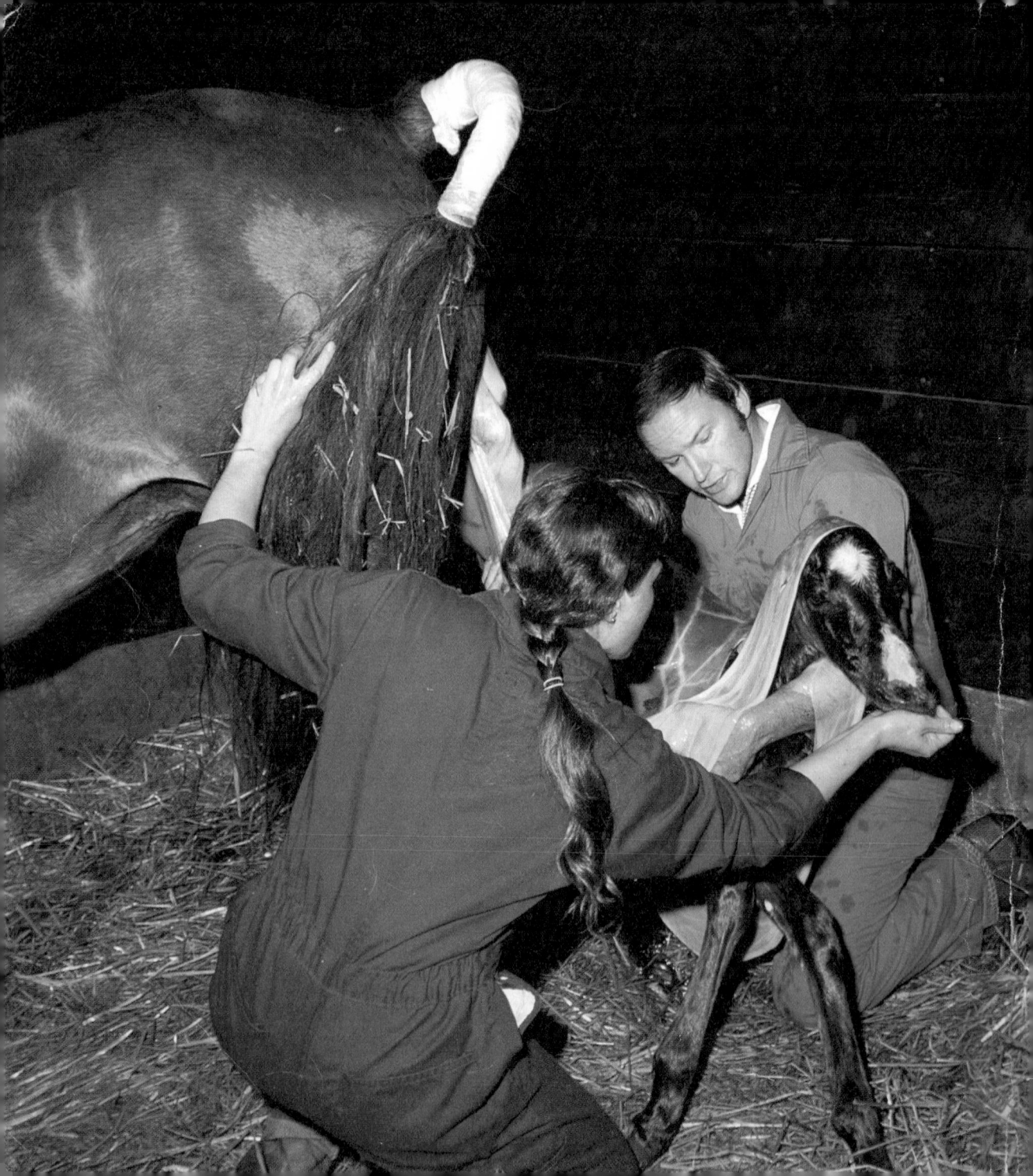

Some mares get help from
people when they give birth.
This baby is still partly covered
by the sac which held him inside
his mother's body.

The mother licks her new baby.

She helps her foal find his first meal.

Life with
Mother

Warm milk makes a strong baby.

Running with
mother builds
strong legs.

It's fun to run with the othe

abies and their mothers, too.

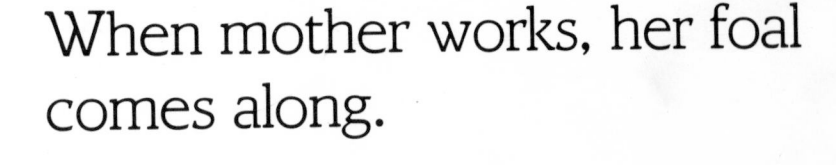

When mother works, her foal
comes along.

Mother is good company.

It's nice to know mother is there when she is needed.

But sometimes it's hard to get her attention.

Being Your Own Boss

Long legs make it hard to eat the sweet, tender grass.

They make it even harder to
lick salty ground.

There's more than one way to
scratch an itch. Sometimes a
hoof will do the job.

Other times,
teeth are the
answer.

Trying to Be
Grown Up

Getting everything to work right isn't easy when you're young.

The spring air smells of grass
and flowers.

Hay is hard to
deal with at first.

Is this bush good to eat?

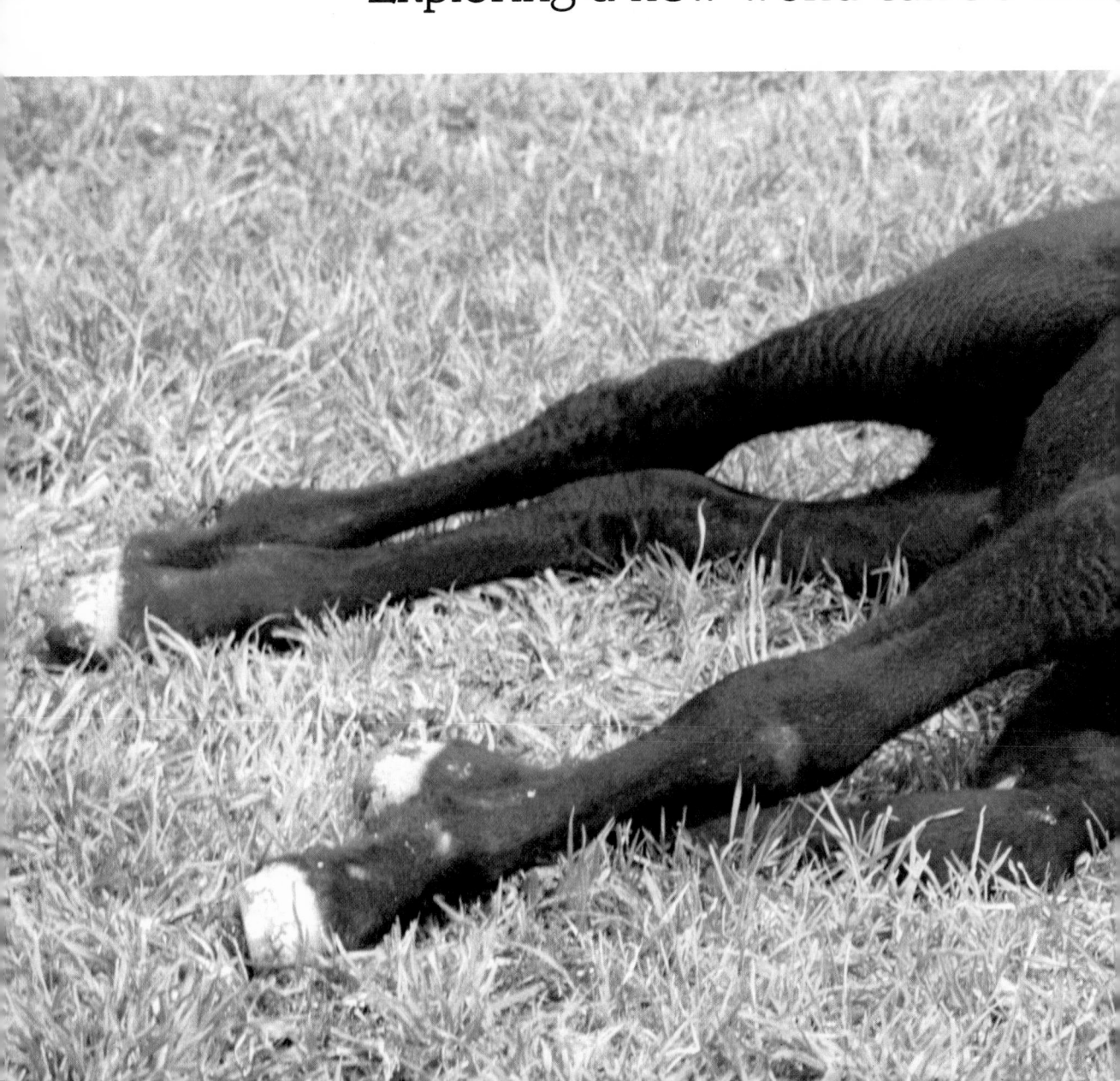

nd babies need their naps.

Friends

As they grow older, foals spend more and more time away from their mothers.

Young horses
have fun exploring
together.

46

They nuzzle each other in greeting.

They nip playfully.

ay with each other.

Like grown-up horses, foals
enjoy grooming one another,
each nibbling the other's fur.

Counting
on Yourself

Foals rear and kick in the brisk morning air.

It's fun to run and jump, even
when you're alone.

But running can
be tiring.

Foals are often curious about the camera.

It doesn't take long to build
strong muscles.

By wintertime,
foals are on their
own. Fuzzy coats
protect them
from the cold.

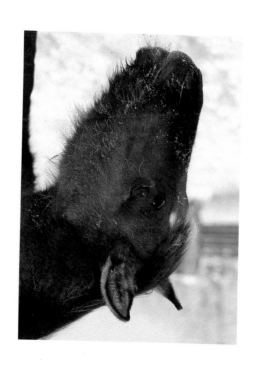